Homes Around the World

Merrily P. Hansen

Sadlier-Oxford
A Division of William H. Sadlier, Inc.

Contents

Some people live where it is very hot.

This home is made of branches.

Some people live where it is very cold.

This home is made of snow.

Some people live where it is very wet.

This home is made of leaves.

Some people live where it is very dry.

This home is made of clay.

Some people live where there are many trees.

This home is made of logs.

Some people live where there are not many trees.

This home is made of grass.

9

Some people live in more than one place.
They take their homes with them!

This home is made of cloth.

My Social Studies Project

Draw Different Homes

What You Need:

crayons   drawing paper

What You Do:

1. Fold a sheet of paper in half.

2. Draw your home on the top.

3. Draw a home from another place on the bottom.

4. Tell how the homes are alike and how they are different.

Index

12